The Monarch Butterfly

Written by Sarah Gaitanos
Photographs by Brian Enting

The monarch butterfly
lays eggs on the leaves
of the swan plant.
The eggs hatch into
little caterpillars.

The little caterpillars start to eat.
They eat the leaves
of the swan plant.

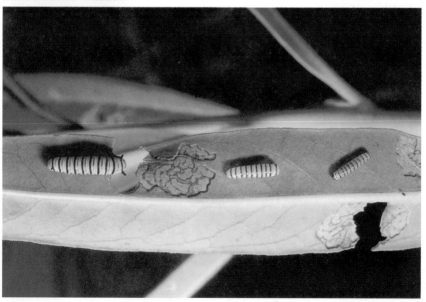

The little caterpillars grow.
They get fat.
They keep on eating.

When they are ready,
they stop eating.
They are ready to pupate.

The caterpillar hangs from a branch
and slips off its coat.

It curls up into the shape of a J.
It changes into a pale green pupa.

For three weeks,
the pupa hangs there.
It has gold spots that shine in the sun.

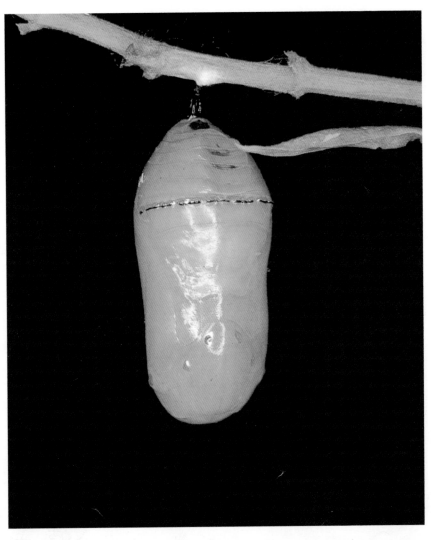

Then it turns black.
The butterfly has formed.
It is ready to hatch.

The butterfly hatches head first.
Its wings are sticky and small—
but not for long.

The next day, it is ready to fly.
It flies from flower to flower
looking for food.

After ten days, it finds a mate.
They fold their wings together,
and several days later,
the female lays lots of little eggs.